Orange Crush

Orange Crush

POEMS Simone Muench

To Julie —
Thanks for your lovely
words. I look forward
to reading your poetry —
Anyone with silver shoes
as cool as yours has to
be A fabulous poet.
with light & music,

[signature]

10/21/10

Sarabande Books
LOUISVILLE, KENTUCKY

FIRST EDITION

Library of Congress Cataloging-in-Publication Data

Muench, Simone, 1969–
    Orange crush : poems / Simone Muench. — 1st ed.
        p.   cm.
    ISBN 978-1-932511-79-6 (pbk. : acid-free paper)
    I. Title.
    PS3563.U358O73 2010
    811'.54—dc22   2009030423

ISBN-13: 978-1-932511-79-6

Cover art: Title Unknown, 1926, Yves Tanguy. Provided courtesy of The Metropolitan
Museum of Art, The Pierre and Maria-Gaetana Matisse Collection, 2002. (2002.456.6)
Image © The Metropolitan Museum of Art. © 2010 Estate of Yves Tanguy/Artists
Rights Society (ARS), New York.

Cover and text design by Charles Casey Martin

Manufactured in Canada
This book is printed on acid-free paper.

Sarabande Books is a nonprofit literary organization.

The Kentucky Arts Council, the state arts agency, supports
Sarabande Books with state tax dollars and federal funding from
the National Endowment for the Arts.

This project is supported in part by an award from The National
Endowment for the Arts.

Contents

Acknowledgments

Many thanks to the editors and staff who first published these poems, sometimes in earlier versions with different titles.

The &Now Awards: The Best of Innovative Writing: "Orange Girl Suite 1,2,3,4"

Best of the Net: "Orange Girl Suite 11"

blossombones: "outline in neon" (starring kimberly l)," "Pages From an Unknown Title (227)"

Caffeine Destiny: "Hex," "Pox"

Cordite Review: "the aperture (starring mackenzie c)," "the bestiary (starring jackie w)," "bachata girl (starring amy f)"

Denver Quarterly: "the femme fatale" (starring sophia k)," "the arsonist (starring brandi h)," "the fever (starring kristy b)"

Iowa Review: "Photograph 3014: Execution of and Unknown Child"

Locuspoint: "Orange Girl Suite 10, 11, 14"

LUNA: "You Were Long Days and I Was Tiger-lined"

Pebble Lake Review: "Bind," "Pages from an Unknown Title (6, 448 and epilogue)"

P.F.S. Post: "an apiary (starring kristy o)," "beetle-beauty (starring lauren l)," "a train track (starring mary b)"

POOL: "Where Does Your Body Rest?," "Count Backwards Toward a Future with You in It," "Chiaroscuro," "With Pendant and Bending Arch," "A Captivating Corset"

Seven Corners: "the ferment (starring jesse m)," "the elliptic mirror (starring lina v)," "the matryoshka (starring hadara b)"

Three Candles: "Psalm," "Orange Girl Suite 5, 7, 8, and 15"

Wicked Alice: "Orange Girl Suite 1, 2, 3, 4, 6, 12"

Write-On: "Orange Girl Suite 9"

Additional thanks to Alhambra Publishing for reprinting "You Were Long Days and I Was Tiger-lined" in the 2008 Alhambra Calendar, "Hex" in the 2009 Calendar and "Orange Girl Suite 1" in the 2010 Calendar; to the PSA and Times Square Alliance for printing "Her Dreaming Feet"; and to Charles Jensen for nominating "Orange Girl Suite 11" for Best of the Net. I am indebted to Nate Slawson, Paula Carey, Vincent Dermody, Andy McFadyen-Ketchum, and Valerie Martt Wallace for reprinting several of these poems. Gratitude and special thanks to Melissa Culbertson and Susan Slaviero of *blossombones;* to the tireless Kristy Bowen of dancing girl press for publishing some of the poems from section two as a chapbook; to the Illinois Arts Council for their support; to Yusef Komunyakaa who will always be one of my oracles; to Dara Wier for her stunning poems and for so graciously volunteering to read my manuscript; and to Sarah Gorham and all those at Sarabande for the beautiful work they do.

Record

"Dear Reader—a lady speaking to humans from
the motion of her own mind is always multiple."
—Lisa Robertson

Hex

Trouble came and trouble
brought greasy, ungenerous things:
poke root and bladderwrack,
chalklines in bloody bedrooms
and black reptilian bags
smelling of acetylene.

Trouble came and trouble sang
shush-shush or tell-tell
for I alone will break your bones
as he bedded down for winter
in a small small town,
smelling of cabbage and tripe
where eight black chickens
wandered the street.

With trouble came clouds
agitating the cows, their thick
ruminant bodies clogging up
the riverbeds. Trouble came
and sang and fish turned belly-up,
house pets appeared in the well.
Children started dying
of oddities the small-town
doctor could not name.

Trouble-houses, trouble-towns.
Trouble came in one hundred waves,

in sparks and hexes, with horse-breath
and spiny borders. Babies born
with clubfoots and cleft lips, babies
born with partial hearts and partial heads
and some just born plain dead.

Trouble is and trouble was
and trouble came and sang
shush-shush or tell-tell
in a small small town.

You Were Long Days and I Was Tiger-Lined

master wear a mask when you break out the leather
the whip's encounter loosens the back to plumage

how strange whip's sibilance moving
through ears like a wet ribbon   harmonium

harpsichord   its lisp then nothingness

it once lived past the pecan orchard   past the barn
where a young girl hung herself in summer

with the reins of her horse   past the river and its stash
of leaves   small animals' waterlogged bodies

master the whip is whispering   birds gather
around her handle   the night thick with red feathers

I am encumbered by the whip's lasciviousness
by the monarchy of your posture   by breath and braid

master you are a totem pole with zapata mustache while my back
is the z-coordinate   pattern on vellum   satsuma plum

the room grows thick with incisions   weather me better master
white votives   and odor of cascarilla float to the river

stutter   startle   wind can carry a whip but how
can a dead girl swerve into flight and miss the sky altogether

A Captivating Corset

We look for refuge but drift to damage,

toward asphyxiation & cord slippage.

Propose, then dispose. In a vaporous season,

half-endings visit the backdoor with frisson.

Is desire a viral captivity? Or, a tender pour

of milk into an infinite glass? A rapport

between flutter & verdict. Cedar

sweetness of skin instructs even as we blur

into blushing clouds, atmospheric, dispersed.

Silk scarves fasten wrists to a dark-tailed bird

windfalling through air, spinning regimes

to bondage narratives, programmed to be

belittled. Surge of marrow when the body bends

toward its own dismantling, toward the hands

unscrolling stockings, limbs complicated &

unbiblical. The nerve burden of our molecular outbreak.

Psalm

Fever-damaged girls
light up in a row. Spells
and vixens and dead calico kittens.
The convent said fire. The fire
said kindness. Kindness
took a victim. Bone
bonnets for the little girls
sleeping, and blue
beds for their snapped
necks. A kiss is a bite
is a bit. Slit in the clouds
above a slit throat. A black
coat and a black glove
went missing.

*

One girl was fallen
in cold golden light. Girl
killed by frost, a man's
hand on her starched
white collar, undone and
saturated with woodburn
while snow descended
like laudanum.

*

Doctor, come quick, the little girls
are sick, their voices muffled
by smoke and wool,
hands and psalms.

Hurry, hurry, it's the eclipse,
the girls aren't breathing
and the chapel is leaking.

Doctor, come quick,
someone's a heretic   someone's a witch.

Count Backward Toward a Future with You in It

for Heye Miyazaki

We slant toward a sprung sun, a rolling
loaded green, but find specks

of cobalt spittle: radiotherapy's blue-
black bulls-eye. We lay down

fixed as wax, let the hospital's
IV & ghost sonata troll through us

while the word we won't speak
flashes its gold-rot teeth. Let's begin

again: we lean into the world's end,
its pink & peach geographies,

into a room with both nurse &
obelisk. Sutured or seamless.

Anything's possible in the attendant day,
hope hums its copper wires

into arms. A hematoma emerges—
rose caterpillar on a woman's chest

where the portacath builds its tumulus,
where the wound contracts & the world

looks less readable. In that tissue
is all that is us. Fissure & tear,

grainy abyss & disappearing
cathedral. The wide wide weather

channel. Nothing prepares us for dying,
not even dying. Nothing separates us

from the sun's luminous text,
the way words enter skin in fire spirals

lilting the room into a red vivarium.
Splinter sung our puckered lips. A kiss

of clouds lingers at the window,
colorless & already past due.

Pox

I am filthy weather
fog-contagious, a spilled liquid
flicker-fade and roughcast

near darkness, near children
near smoke, near wing
near lips, near listen

conflagrations in vain
crowd-crime

will rise at midnight
will flourish
will find you

a perdition, a constellation
vertigo's torsion

will wring
will displace
will spin into the city

to be pretty
to be waiting
to be answered

at the city's main gate
undertakers play
backgammon

would they stay otherwise
blackwashed and fire-winged
scarred by starfall.

Where Does Your Body Rest?

for the woman who said I lacked duende while undergoing chemo and radiation

The weather signed the guest book
& left us bereft. Told we'd never
be loved, we nightmared together.
Noise webbed its way through

as we imagined slinging peach pits
into the river, dreaming of green
light & luck & chainsaws.
The tender windmills of hands.

Maria, we speak with black slats
& spun sugar as we swerve
to the grit, grinding our eyes
into tomorrow's shadow cast.

We play the game of blankness.
Are we to be late carrion
in a late century, a post-it
note on a disintegrating object,

a colossal flame that bends
to its own heat, a clean
cotton nightgown with yellow bows
that signals disease for lease?

Maria, you say we have
no blackness, we're silk

stockings, so transparently nude.
Our skin strung between fever tree

& error. Your guess is gilded frame:
say *portrait* or *perishable*,
& still you wouldn't know
insomnia from enamored.

You say we have no *via dolorosa*,
but cup your ear, Maria,
to the gear slippage in our voices,
stranded in this artic dark.

And where are you now, Maria,
why won't you answer our knock?

Photograph 3014: Execution of an Unknown Child

Frame 1

Your hands
open like your mouth.
Arc lamp of eye; terrible
engine of your head.
A counterrevolutionary at 13.
Colt wedded to your coat: a wool-wet
path of moths.

Record of reach,
of fingers and waiting.
Low voices behind
closed oak doors.

Frame 2

The Kittlerian camera
shoots you as you gaze
straight into the cylindrical
barrel of a pistol. Record
breath: blink.

Transport of pictures repeats
the transport of bullets.

Frame 3

Record of a clock your father once
pitched at your head. You vaguely
remember the ticking. Silk
stockings, metal
burn of a gun, a mew gull
flying out of reach.

Record of trees
pierced by shrapnel.

Frame 4

Record of the executed.
Record of an aperture.
Record of etiquette.
Record of a cold sea.

Frame 5

Faint glitter of black coffee.
A ring of dead men, vanishing.

Can I? What if? You waited.
Record of vital organs.

You slept in the earth
to avoid the stars.

Tired of light and galaxies,
tired of men and milk,

so tired, you whispered
behind the full-length mirror

that reflected moon-blue moths
but not your missing form.

Frame 6

The Colt sang once, parting
your pitch dark hair.
Flesh turns to sugar. Grey gull
swallows the sound. Its
silver wingtip, clipped by light,
glitters insistently. Feathers
turn to sea reflections.

Record of your smell.
Sun-wet. Songfleck.

Rehearsal

... orange girls (~1660–1700) were considered little better than prostitutes, and success depended as much on a girl's looks as on her line of patter.

—HRH Princess Michael Of Kent, 2006

Are you lonely and looking for hot sexy girls in orange?

—spam, 2008

Orange Girl Suite

1:
Young women carrying baskets of oranges used to stand near the stage in
London theatres and sell oranges at sixpence apiece and themselves for little more

between dresses we came.
between naked and nothing
we slipped into the delirious
coils of perfected ears,

      pear dust on our skin
           sarsparilla sounding our
                  fizzied song in sailor mouths.

we were translated by churchwomen
who placed umlauts over our words,

when we recovered, we were sold
in beautiful clothes, sent sailing into the gulf
where the moon pitched
its lemon-lateness over the celluloid

      slickness of sea. we were movie stars
           who never entered the frame.
               we were green and gone

lisping "o" words in the air:
ode, odalisque, obituary.

2:

The rynde of the orrendge is hot, and the meate within it is cold

there are only two ways
        to peel an orange
                in fragments or in one
        coiling brightness.
let us rewind and revel
        in the orangeade of sun-
                decked eyes. turn me spinning
        in a carousel-sweet dress
ear marked by radio teeth
        red leaf breath.
                your arm is on fire
        as we ride in a dark
car to the carnival.
        the constant clink
                of seatbelt to belt buckle.
        the sky's cotton candy
melting in a girl's cold mouth.

3:
*The orange-girl is generally allowed to enter an auction-store, for auctioneers
are mortal, and sometimes eat oranges*

I'm stone and pulp, like policemen's wives.
you're emerald, buried in dark clothes.
your eyes leaf, bone.

your fingers so many songs

out of tune

I have fallen out of trees singing your name; I have
fallen into your foliation

into your moth-mouth, plum-
thick tongue.

wherever you are, I'll be white teeth,
an abandoned town, a wrapped parcel.

I'll be a blonde in a black smock with sex
appeal, smelling of apiaries.

I'll be a cold sea in an old war film.
I'll be insubordinate

and seville sweet.

you'll be long gone
though you said you'd never leave
those poor crippled orange trees.

4:
The soft night-wind went laden to death with flowering orange scent

tongues harvest petals, larvae
the back of the throat is petticoat pink
the girl in the dirty dress is dead

I wish I were a fish lit by phosphorescence
I wish I were in Spain
I wish I were blue-gilled and beautiful

a man folds the girl up in newspapers
her wet hair a string of taffy, a rope, something
unraveling inside the man's eye

when he killed her he said *listen*
when he killed her he said
your soul, orange girl

he said *windowsill*
he said *stone*
while alive she replied

oilslick, doorjam. something
passing through my right eye:
black cars and carousels

pretty maids all in a row

5:
Where there's bush orange, there's a fault line, and where there's a fault line, there's water

a woman knows clementines,
emergency. how crepe myrtle

blossoms stick to a wet face,
a hammer shatters the patella.

cities fire their lights up at night,
a semblance of protection

against the oily darkness, against
animals water-logged in the bay.

disease of a body syntactically
disarranged. limbs and hair

webbed with algae. a silk
dress shadow-spread

across water. a dress
designated for dance, thin

as cocktail napkins. her
own skin gathering the Baltic's

debris, an intersection of earrings
and quiet, wrists and ropes.

somewhere in the pitch
is a song, but the current's

so strong only the drowned
can decipher it.

6:
Orange thickets drip with fruit bright as headlamps

the girl is running, is bleeding, is listening.
the railroad a rusted zipper
fusing Louisiana and Arkansas
into a black cerement of broken trees.
air thick as albumen. a caterwaul
of electricity through phone lines
leads her forward. she is moving
through the woods in a thin
white suture. cusp of the country
singed alizarin. she is passing through
her own life. she runs through rain
until she is rain. her lips suck and crush,
open for windrush, wordrush.
her body once well-dressed in a small town,
her face now a shadowgraph
beneath her killer's hand.

7:

At each end of the table, a marmalade gelatin mermaid bathed in a brass basin
of orange-flower water

no one can be reached
in this city of correct syntax

where water deposits its marginalia.
this city of aqueducts and evening gowns

sweeping the cobblestones. a girl
dragged along the waterfront,

dropped in a dumpster wearing
a yellow shawl and pearl earrings,

her hair once smelling of pears
and held by tortoiseshell, now covered

in banana spiders, greasy eggshells.
this city closes its windows to the odor

and forgets that a girl went missing,
forgets any girl who "got herself strangled."

the canal said body. the body said murder.
murder said get me a witness while I wait

for a soft-armed girl carrying fruit
and soup to her sick mother. this city

is thick with cold cases and ripped pantyhose,
ligature marks and headlines blaming women

for wearing short skirts after dark.

8:

The orange had been squeezed, and the rind thrown to rot in the highway

smell of cash and mouthwash
complete the stunted summer day.
so does a maggot in a wound,

devouring. are you a highway robber
or a housewife? do you dream
of beetles or green snakes, rare
steak or heirloom tomatoes?

everything is monstrous today. hot
blossoms in the night. wood or wound.

knives desire and humidity dissolves
clothes off neighbors
who know something is not right

but close their curtains and blur
behind oldies and air-conditioning.

next door a man is staring at a body.
next door a man is carving a body

while his neighbors smile,
offer bourbon on the back porch
where July is hot with sand and orange
compote, sinister sweetness.

9:
A cause betweene an orendge wife, and a forset-seller

hunter, I hand you
a red sweater, whisper
of precipitation.

trigger-happy laughter
in the light-latticed
forest. you burn

my nightgown
to undergrowth
in this feral

season. overseer
to all small
deaths, your lips

an orange smear
of cordiality.
your rifle's leverage

cocks your spine.
my skin is soft.
the safety's off.

10:
*The mirror cracks from top to bottom like an orange made in the image of
my sister*

at the love hotel she lost her legs
intersection of table and torso
her pockmarked face pretty

and blue like violet pastilles
so sweet   so dead
so divine a cadaver

a pearl comb beside her head
smell of eggs and gin drifting
red ribbons around her wrist

she was looking out of herself
through so many stabmarks, eye slits
so many voyeured holes

camera flash on her mouth
her belly, a billfold
zoom

to navel
vortex of torso
vertigo

*

who lit the lamps this evening
who lit the girl
with windex and gasoline

she is glass, she is straw
she is waiting for us
to wake up through her eyes

her wounds deep as waistcoats
her eyes umbrellas, her eyes
ghost open like milk in a mason jar

her no, her no, her lilac dress
her wrists, her lips, her darting tongue
at the love hotel she says goodbye.

11:
To give a child an idea of scarlet or orange, of sweet or bitter, I present the
objects

in the spider-broke shack on the edge
of the metropolis,

in the song of the red canary,
city listens   city bends

its avenues to hear smitten
girls in floral nightgowns

sleeping next to coal light
with moth vibrations

drawing up their legs.

murder moves us
through autumn months.

the girl buried in her
mother's best holiday dress.

her body now swelling
into puberty underground.

       pear, petal, razor, torture
       smell of lemondrops

her dread of blue balloons.

12:

I never was an orange girl; but I have the gutter in my blood all right

sweater girl, elevator girl,
factory girl unsnarling her pin curls,
gibson girl, varga girl

au pair girl, bunny girl, flower girl,
career girl, chorus girl, college girl,
cover girl, geisha girl, party girl

wayward girl, servant girl, bachelor girl,
campfire girl, working girl, give-it-a-whirl girl,
bar girl, call girl, check girl, farm girl

shop girl, street girl,
sausage curl girl,
poor girl, you speak like a green girl

between two girls, which hath the merriest eye?
flint and pearl alike
my cold cold girls!

13:

Till all the crimson changed, and past into deep orange o'er the sea

the water owns her, wears her
like a blue ball gown embossed

with froth. cypress swoon
in white light. leaves fall

into goldfish. beneath a boat,
a girl. beneath the girl, a poppy

spilling into fire-tangles, into
a balefire wheeling on the water.

                    in one version, she folds up

like a fan, her songs pleated
gills panting underwater.

in another, she fashions
the wires of her earrings

into antennae, transmitting
her story across the harbor,

her taffeta dress sliding
toward the lighthouse without her.

14:

Have you seen that place along the waterfront where they sell orange crush?

a scar like a sea-bird
floats over your forearm,
salt-stenched breezes
recall oblivion and bone
barrettes. too much wine
and china oranges lead us
sternward, though we know
nothing of the nautical.
we are at home with avenues,
asphalt. the butcher shop
on the corner where the *chop-*
chop of blade to meat is
oddly comforting in the morning
when the sun is gorged
with pollen light and the small
red blossoms of geraniums
blow along the marquees
and boarded up store-fronts.

somewhere, the sound of flesh
and flower, a woman is
lost, laughing.

15:

She slipped out of the Moorish gate and into the orange grove

on days when the air is sea-
water taffy and glittering

surfaces are coated in kerosene,
one refrains from saying "bedclothes"

for fear of causing hospitals
and courthouses to flame,

a proliferating scarlet,
an utterance uncontained.

summer and sentences trickle
down our backs as we gather

driftwood from the river
to build a house

that cannot hold us.
like riddles and diseases

we are a multiplying sigh.
we are fevered with fervor

and red liqueur. the wax
of sealed envelopes. the fact

is we disappear as departing
footsteps, orange girls

blazing through doors
of sugarwater and fire.

Recast

I say my power, should be *our* power.
—Buffy

(we hadn't been cursed or blessed) (we'd been syncopated)
—Dara Wier

Orange Girl Cast

1: the fever

(starring kristy b)

Sweet Kristy of the culvert, the ankle turn, the verb imperfect, and sailors' notebooks. In this metropolis of binoculars and chicken bones, in this city black with chicken-wire alchemists and bloody gutters, she feigns a fever in her red brassiere, her lavender dress lilting across headlights of chrome sedans: skin livid-exquisite with light bulbs and batteries beneath sinister-shouldered men, zombie drunk from fermented peaches and her silk stocking smell. Sweet Kristy of the corset, born of Anne Boleyn and a bird collector, born of alum and blindfolds, born to unzip men's breath, their clamorous wrists with an alphabet on her breast, a switchblade pinned to her taffeta thigh. Where are you leading with your eyelets and hooks, catching men with clothespins and rain in the perfect sphere of your dance hall mouth.

2: the femme fatale

(starring sophia k)

She says, *It's true*. The rain of her inside men's homes from fishtail to foreplay. Blue-black myth of her rapturous hair, corkscrewing letters of lovers' names: the gate of E, filigree of J. She's not winter sweet minutiae, she's iridescent yellow, a meteorite. You can't fold her up inside like a cocktail napkin. She will not rinse. She's Mexican flowers blazing from an idol's mask. The snow boy and owl who live by the river gather round her immaculate star-studded slingbacks, as she signs the reflection of her shook foil loneliness.

O swayback bather. Don't blame her. She suffers you like cheap champagne; like sex on an airplane. Full of bright wings and woodcuts, she's the pink T-bird's flush&flash. A wineglass filled with fight. Some murmuring man plump with past damage thinks it would be nice to end up in a small town where she leaks her song, asking for sarsaparilla. She's no odalisque in organza, she imprisons pharaohs in her spine. She is a woman who will not stutter, an apple of Peru. In her magnolia latticed teeth, a dollhead floats free of *I do*.

3: the arsonist

(starring brandi h)

Her calendar charm kick-starts men's lips while her wrists drip with doorbells. When the doctor gazed at her, a nurse parade passed in his head. Thread of alizarin through her hair. She revs her engine with stars and white thigh-highs, while choirboys chant *holy, holy* in the burlesque of her hip swing. Though she was born at a roadblock, her legato knees open for the congregation. Murmur of campfire under her hair. Murmur of bass notes, rubber gloves. *Sugar*, she says, *my lips are firebrands that'll make your gold cross vibrato.* The boys saw in prescribed light, her thorned orbit. Her breath full of footprints and soporific ruin. Her arm an empty room.

4: the train track
(starring mary b)

Train track flutter girl; coriander lips and Prohibition ale. That empty mouth like a bottle on a man's neck. Marabou soft, doe's muzzle on a pomegranate split, ultraviolet. You might have to rid yourself of all the boys, mostly rapscallions. How they feel under hands: red fish, big branches caught in your rain-rinsed hair, river tresses. For your ankle, a thread of nine carat bone. While the crossbuck sign bells with danger, citronella girls smoke Parliaments with a felon; your campfire jaw, a kerosene swoon.

5: bachata girl
(starring amy f)

Days full of breastmilk and weathervanes. Odor of damp wigs and the body's brachial splintering. The river settles in her mouth as mornings splay before her with egg-cups capsizing, a doll torn in half in her hands. She grounds down into routine but when the UPS man approaches, her feet remember Miami, bachata, stilettos. A table-breaking high kick. She is lodged in the beat of one stray finger against a jawbone.

Against static-broken stations, she can't remember the song her mother used to sing. Something about the egg-and-butter man buttering up his sugar plum. She hears wolves rain-howl and families brawl as she dreams her way toward Florida's pale noon netting. Holding a handkerchief up to the changing light's narrative, its clovered air. Her eyes full of thread, dark as seaweed.

6: the ferment

(starring jesse m)

Fever-lit and gin-livid, she says, *wring the nightshade from my eyes. Let me be an explosion.* Thorned and hooved, slipping in swampwater in a brackish March gone mad, in a shuttered house against a backdrop of fish bones and lace chemises spread across the lawn. Bullet something for biting as midnight visits with waterlogged lungs and bird carcasses. The swamp tests the distance when entire dialects go missing. *I am* floats by, dangling in a line of light bulbs while wisteria shapes the atmosphere; stanzas etched into lavender soap and peaches she'd wrap in gauze. A seed to let the body speak. One mason jar, one wineglass, a murder and a verb. The beat of unsettle in her song.

7: beetle-beauty
(starring lauren l)

Through fossils of grapefruit, her words full of climacteric Kafka sadness.
Night moths rest in her carnelian desert. There I found her fire-tossed hair,
jade green horns and bowed down to a bonfire beauty. Her father left her
a blanket by the bedroom wall between a cigar and a scream. The mustard-
colored house lost beyond a pepper tree. The curtains, like carapaces, and
a mad rushing descent as if to name an object: long and shedding its
scabbed horizon, a *Chalcosoma caucasus* at the limits of her frame.

8: the apiary
(starring kristy o)

We drink in strange trades, skålling over your chest of bees. What would you choose—red meat or Coco Chanel? Gentle violence or violent tenderness? When reading Keats, we bloomed gold thighs, pink sadnesses. At your bedroom window, you leaned toward refuge into moth wings. Outside, our black eyes, transparent sting. You said, *hello, blank-eyed, zero in*! Our home base, a distant cabana; our family secrets stitched like a honeycomb riddled by jimsonweed. Old fictions born of red letter afflictions and the redivivus of southern cypress. When the light gonged, we slipped into the attic, and you became a foehn whispering through the veils of glamorous biblical women, loaded up on blossom.

9: the elliptic mirror
(starring lina v)

At the far side of barely, there is no reaching her mouth, her parabolic ear. She is an undertow of linen with a lakeside cadence. When the doctor diagnosed blindness, she heard rain, and from thenceforth the world was wet. The sky plump with milk and lunation. Moving between gardenia beam and umbra, her face upturns. Radiates silver convexity. Her eyes ever apogee, not apology.

10: outline in neon
(starring kimberly l)

A girl leans across a counter, edges of her hair flaring neon. She is a verb written on a cardboard marquis. Aluminum moon, savior of nightjars. Her scar a red glass cardinal. Where did the country take her sun-tipped bangs? Her girlhood diminishing in Sunday school hymns. Our lady of the unsaluted past. Lady of cornhusks & sericulture, arrowheads & fruit bats. Smelling of upholstery, she falls bird-winged into intramuscular structures, a blueprint of sutures inside an inaudible mouth. Architecture of insinuations. Black hiss of asphyxiation. What is this equation prickling through her like chicory? Limned in language or bondage. Her frame made strange, goldleafed, and dangerously askew.

11: the matryoshka
(starring hadara b)

Sunlight buzzes your windows into being as you crack a kaleidoscope in half, searching for a photograph of your mother before disease splits her face into reflection and recollection. When you slide to the floor, your dress spreads volcanic; an orange silk corona framing the hands' flawless architecture, the fire-station in your stomach. An invisible fretwork of sutures keeps you intact though you are known to leak milkglass and bandages inscribed with epigraphs.

Above, the sun falls feather-slow into the sea; familial passage from flame to salt water. Your eyes etched in a black forest; nerve cells spinning their way into the emptiness that holds half your body, while your mother calls *daughter* with a seagrass sad languor, settling into the somatic bed you've carved out for her; a nested doll, her face behind your face, safeguarded. Humming you into your own existence.

12: the bestiary

(starring jackie w)

In a tongue-snap sky, waxwings unspool over the plains. He was a whisper, she was Nebraska. Her hands pepperweed, pebble, pearl to pearl, so tone-smooth. Her mouth speaks, a red canary to a dime cigar. Spittle sheen. There are worse things than being a pretty Catholic girl without any guilt.

She gives herself over to the music, embracing the Phoenician sailor and swearing beneath the cinema screen. Under the ostinato, under the train's rustle, she goes down. With her topaz neck and her bestiary lure. With her coloratura and vixen gene, she goes down. Into the musk and hum and howl.

O lady of the bossa nova. O girl born of semaphores. Into the moss and phosphorous. Into the salt marsh and subjunctive silence. With currants in her mouth, a yellow scarf around her neck, she goes.

13: the aperture
(starring mackenzie c)

Flash-faced. A tailspin of squares. There in photographs, footprints lead to a window with a green fog vista, heavy with ears. Gypsum lines the driveway where houses replicate themselves. She can't see her way out of this syntax, out of window sashes, this fretted light where blossoms slide to brambles & a woman is shorn of her hair. Follicular. Glistening. Her spine spun honey. Iridescence means eggplant, means isinglass.

Her pulse quartzing.

Where do we go from here? Morphemes dangle in her injury. A pinafore on the floorboard of the car, and she's speeding away. Moving between white-wash & crosshatch. Between syllable & windshield. Seeding the helix of distances. A snowball capturing light in versions of her.

Redress

All of us girls have been dead for so long.
But we're not going to be anymore.
—Kathy Acker

With Pendant and Bending Arch

She's a washed-out blue smock, hungering
for a good month. Itching with naphthalene,
the margins of mouth: fuse of dead to deed
awed to weird   shin to sheen.

He's Ouspensky-driven, a science-fiction
slipstream. Jacaranda tree in lean dark clothes,
sipping silver-fizzes. His body
iron-pyrite   globed gaslight.

Lightning, lips, treachery.
A riddle is linked to her pink lipstick.
No one is without stories, she says.

She commutes between his hands
and the faint sweet scent of bakery shelves.
You have my face:
a chasm, imagine.

Dialing his large white teeth
with her tanager-tongue,
she laments, *Where art my thigh?*

Skip it, sugar, he says. *I slept miserably.*
Running from myself in Barcelona.

Ask the strange man on adrenalin reserves—
would a maniac roam around a cemetery
wearing one black glove?

Ask the vexed readers
what they really want: creature
or clone, a romance between cousins,
zombies behind the shower curtain?

Ask yourselves in the ice cube
light of an effervescing cocktail:
What happens to skin when its language is limited?
What happens to the elusive rabbit, its alien magic?

Ask the music.
Ask the sheerest silk stockings.

Her Dreaming Feet

Sketched in quotation marks, Times Square flares aortic in the bee-
bronzed dark. Broadcast of vendors & shoulders bustling with cannon
percussion in the retinal ring out of peignoir signage. A harmony
of women swim in the aquarium-fluorescence, unlined linen

dresses translucent beneath the yellow & claret lights. Compass
of this square fizzied orange soda sadness. Like gold teeth submerged
in a glass of green tea, a scrim between the lenticular & surreal—noble gas
marquees shift in the drizzle from flamingo to bordeaux, converge

with human activity, an arcade for the conspicuously need-to-be-kissed.
But digital billboards of nightgowns won't hold us up when tenderness
turns to concept & is backswept from view. No more aerialist
tricks to resist, so the conductor retires to the wilderness

while the city smoke-stitched with bluing alleys writes its own discography
& lights buzz out a new alphabet, divine a new topography.

Bind

One drowned bride is an accident.
Two drowned brides is suspicious.
Three drowned brides is murder.
                    —law document

1:
Honeycombs fall
        into the lake.
                Spillage of bodies
        bogged down by the viscosity
where bee meets algae.

Amidst a cage of drowned brides
        there is one who floats
                free. Her veil still attached
        drags her upward
into warmer water.

Mesh nets fall idly from boats.
        The fish have eaten, are drunk
                on honey and the teeth
        of old combs that fill
the versal lake.

The green spine of the dock
        bows with rot. Beneath
                a bevy of girls
        who once sang in the choir,
now wet doilies

growing filigree. Flesh
	separates. Its duration
		shadow-slack.

"Loup off the steed," says false Sir John,
"Your bridal bed you see;
For I have drowned seven young ladies,
The eighth one you shall be.

2:
We vertigo sweetly
	into the sea
		while lights flicker at the shoreline.
	We are falling beneath a lit mirror.
We are ghosts in Victorian gowns,
	lilac apparitions with parasols,
		black reticules.
	The water whispers its waves in our brain.
The water draws our voile dresses down.
	We screamed once and then
		were muffled.

"Cast off, cast off, my May Colven,
All and your silken gown,
For it's oer good and oer costly
To rot in the salt sea foam.

3:
We sit beneath the sea
	like good girls in hard pews

while water rivulets our faces
with numerals. We are bone clocks
ticking. We are skin undone by
the ocean's need for archivists.

Through a ship's periscope, we appear
moonfaced and shy beneath the tide.
Sitting on our suitcases
we wave lace handkerchiefs
adding light to the oceanic green, but

when sailors and map-makers
return to the crime, we tie their ropes
in half-hitches, leave them
sinking as we sing new shanties
and climb the rungs of the sea:

"No help, no help, O false Sir John,
No help, nor pity thee;
Tho' seven kings' daughters you have drownd,
But the eighth shall not be me.

Pages from an Unknown Title

page 6:

Nervous spiders on a copper
pipe. An arm. An anklet
in the well. Find
your way out of this
deathmess, Baby. You are blued
& dappled by the crosstown's
light. Gardenias steam
your skin in the aftermath
of Southland dreams. You were
never meant to be

glamorous cake
on the table for stuffed
diners. You were a brilliant wink,
a prosperous dilettante
sidestepping your way
out of small towns
& their Georgio residue.

Belt buckles tightened
your way to a wet grave.
Now you blink blue
icing eyes. When you bent
your spine, you bent
this town in two.

page 227:

In a jar overflowing
with Atlas moths, the smell

    of breastmilk & bayous
    overtakes the instrument of eye:

In a world sketched on a wing,
there was silverware & automata,

    a girl drowning
    in a vat of molasses,

there was a pair of red satin slippers
tacked to a mannequin,

    Dali's ocelot taxidermied
    & strung up in a freight elevator.

Not believing that peripheries
held more than dioramas, more

    than Louisiana & nectarines,
    you were always sinking

& I was always breathing your lungs
into being. Seeing was for the eagles,

    something beyond trees, something
    beyond this cyclorama of *we.* All those

unbuttoned blouses,
falling leaves.

Soldiers of Robespierre
with frostbite & lice
inch closer to my collarbone.
I'm a ghost vowel
to your bone parade.
Where are the watchtowers
& the men smelling of gunpowder?
Where are the girls with their blizzard hair
& foaming skirts?

Where is your machete?

Why aren't you on the level,
my soldier, my narcotic
worse than a worm-filled ear.
The mulch makes its own music.

I'm disembarking on a blue boat.
My thighs   keels parted
while you pantomime on the shore
in armor & white labcoat
holding a syringe meant for me.

But I'm adrift, no longer
your delivery.

page 720:

A bluebird perches at the edge of eyelids,
flipping its wings into dreams.
We were once lithographs smeared
with inked-chapped hands, now we are
smooth and inscrutable as bone china
without bread or blackberry jam.

Be a serrated knife to softness.
Be a bangle bracelet to a broken arm.
I will chew your light into miniature suns
and when the time comes to bury you,
I will say undo. Undone.

epilogue:

So many girls to break
before nightfall, so many
silhouettes to rearrange.

You think *mantis, eclipse.*

While you fumble her flesh
beneath leopard-skin coat,
she pockets your wallet

with goldleaf fingers,
an exclamation
and the briefest

of dances.

Glitter of a black snakeskin purse
in the unrecoverable distance.

Chiaroscuro

wordlight. sealight. teethlight.
the darkness still visits
us with bad names in bad places

places we escaped when
people said "hoodlum"
& "sweater girl"

girl, don't regret the way
the light tears your dark hair
into highlights, into lumen lines

lines are a way to divide
the seamen from the landmen
saddles from horses

horses gather at the shore
their thickness silhouetted by
moon's loose light & reflection

reflected in the sea
is the reversal of yourself
a smudge in the vastness

vast is a word the sea owns
beneath it your shadow shines

Notes and Dedications

The italicized titles of the Orange Girl Suite are extracted from the OED.

The italicized lines in "Bind" are from the "May Colvin" ballad. Arthur Quiller-Couch, ed. (1863–1944). The Oxford Book of Ballads. 1910.

The Orange Girl Suite is dedicated to Susannah Chase (1974–1997) and my mother Loretta McSween, who's been through hell and still remains one of the kindest people I know.

The women starring in Orange Girl Cast are friends, who are also poets, whom I admire and owe thanks: Hadara Bar-Nadav, Kristy Bowen, Ariana-Sophia Kartsonis, Brandi Homan, Mary Biddinger, Amy Fetzer-Larakers, Kimberly Lojek, Lauren Levato, Kristy Odelius, Lina Ramona Vitkauskas, Jackie White, Jesse Muench, and Mackenzie Carignan. The Orange Girl Cast is dedicated to them as well as to all women, who in Adrienne Rich's words, "are stumbling up the hill hand in hand, stumbling and guiding each other over the scarred volcanic rock." Thanks for your luminous, musical guidance.

Special thanks and colossal gratitude to Hadara Bar-Nadav for her editing deftness and support, and to Jackie White who managed to read and provide insight on this manuscript while putting in a 70-hour work week.

Love and immeasurable thanks to my friends and collaborators who've inspired and supported me (I feel lucky every day to be in the same world with them): Kim Ambriz, Richard Every, Philip Jenks, Lana Rakhman, Catherine Blauvelt, John McSween, Tom Lynch, Francesco Levato, Jason Koo, Jessi Lee Gaylord, Sarah Long, Melissa Grubbs,

Gabert Farrar, Greg Purcell, Jay Reed, Tim Rutili, Joshua Clover, Bill Allegrezza, Ray Bianchi, Jennifer Rupert, Michael Anania, Anne Winters, Reg Saner and Youki. And my unending love and debt to Lanko Miyazaki, Stephanie McCanles, and Bill Mondi for whom I can never dedicate enough books.

The Author

Simone Muench is author of *Lampblack & Ash* (Kathryn A. Morton Prize; Sarabande, 2005), which was named by *The New York Times Book Review* as an "Editor's Choice" selection, and *The Air Lost in Breathing* (Marianne Moore Prize; Helicon Nine, 2000). Her newest chapbook, co-written with Philip Jenks, is *Little Visceral Carnival* (Cinematheque, 2009). She acts as an editor for Sharkforum, serves on the advisory boards of Switchback Books and UniVerse, and is a recipient of two Illinois Arts Council Fellowships, the PSA's Bright Lights/Big Verse Prize, and other awards. Raised in the South, she now lives in Chicago and directs the Writing Program at Lewis University where she teaches creative writing and film studies. She is a vegetarian and a horror film fan.

Richard Every